SIMPLE SCIENCE SAYS:
Take One Compass

by Melvin Berger

Illustrated by
G. Brian Karas

SCHOLASTIC INC.

New York   Toronto   London   Auckland   Sydney

ISBN 0-590-42384-3

Text copyright © 1990 by Melvin Berger.
Illustrations copyright © 1990 by Scholastic Inc.
All rights reserved. Published by Scholastic Inc.

12 11 10 9 8 7 6 5 4 3 2 1   0 1 2 3 4 5/9

Printed in the U.S.A.   11

First Scholastic printing, February 1990

Contents

Jet plane pilots use it.
Ship captains use it.
Explorers use it.
Hikers use it.

What is "it"?

"It" is a compass!

4

A compass shows direction.
Suppose you're lost in the woods.
You might walk in circles — unless you had a compass.
Let's say you're on a long bike trip.
A compass can help you find your way.

This book comes with a tiny compass.
It works just like a big compass,
but it is small enough
to tuck away in some secret place.
(Be careful not to lose it!)

Your tiny compass has a round case and a clear cover.
Inside is a metal pointer.
The pointer is called a needle.
The needle can turn freely.
It jiggles around even when you hold it still.

Under the needle is the compass card.
Printed on it are four large letters—N, E, S, and W.
You probably know what each letter stands for:

    N is north.
    E is east.
    S is south.
    W is west.

North, east, south, and west are
the four main directions. They are called
the cardinal points of the compass.

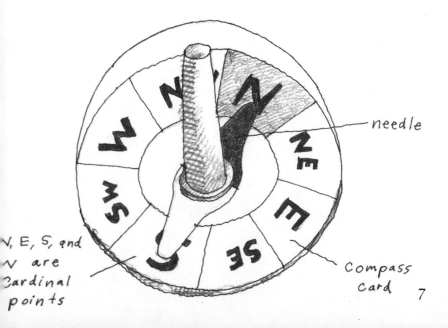

needle

N, E, S, and
W are
Cardinal
points

Compass
Card

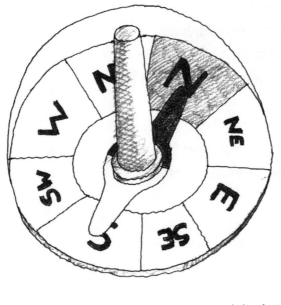

NE, SE, SW, and NW
are intercardinal
points

You can see other letters in between N, E, S, and W.
   Between N and E is NE, or northeast.
   Between E and S is SE, or southeast.
   Between S and W is SW, or southwest.
   Between W and N is NW, or northwest.

NE, SE, SW and NW are the main
intercardinal points of the compass.

To use the compass, hold it flat in your hand.
Be sure the needle can turn easily.

Keep your hand steady.
You'll see the needle swing back and forth.
In a few seconds it will stop moving.
If the needle is stuck,
tilt the compass one way or the other.

Look for the red end of the needle.
The red end points to the north.
No matter where the needle stops, the red end points north.

Is the red end over N on the compass card?
Probably not.
But you can line up the N with the needle.

It's easy.
Slowly turn the compass with your other hand.
Keep turning it until the letter N
is under the red end of the needle.
Now both the needle and the compass card
are facing north.

Follow the needle.
Is it pointing toward a window? A door? A picture on the wall?

Anything in that direction is north.
If you go north far enough, you'll end up at the
North Pole!

Remember, the needle always points north.
No matter what you do, the needle points
in the same direction.
Try it out.

Turn around and face a new direction.
What happens to the red end of the needle?
It swings back and forth for a while.
But then it points north.
It points to the same window, door,
or picture on the wall.

Once you know north you can find
all the other directions. Let's do it!

Which way is south?
Hold the compass still.
Wait for the needle to stop swinging.
Turn the compass until the point marked *N*
is under the red end of the needle.

Now look at the compass card.
Do you see the *S* for south?
It is under the other end of the needle.
South is the direction opposite from north.

Can you find east?
Make sure the *N* is under the red end of the needle.
Look for the letter *E*.
That direction is east.

Try finding some other directions.
Twist the compass so that
N is under the red end of the needle.
Then look for the direction you want.

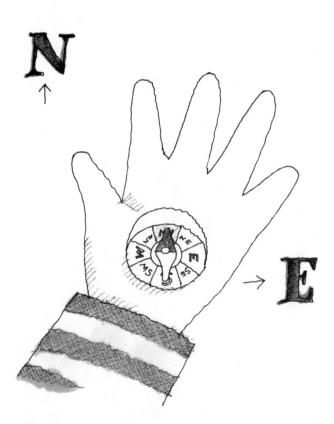

SIMPLE SCIENCE SAYS:
Be a compass cop.

A traffic cop can send cars in all directions.
A compass cop can point in all directions.

Take your compass outside.
(But don't stand in the road!)

Hold the compass in your hand
until the needle stops swinging.
Now turn and face the same direction as the needle.
Which direction are you facing?
North — of course!

Don't move from this spot.
But put the compass away.

You're now ready to be a compass cop.

Point directly ahead of you.
That way is north.

Next point directly behind you.
That direction is south.
South is always opposite from north.

Raise your right arm and point to the right.
This time you're pointing east.

Finally, point to the left with your left arm.
Can you guess which direction that is?
It's west.
West is on your left side.
It is opposite from east.

Always remember this:
When you are facing north —
    — north is in front of you.
    — south is behind you.
    — east is to your right.
    — and west is to your left.

SIMPLE SCIENCE SAYS:
Experiment with your compass.

Look around the room.
Can you tell which things are made of iron?
A pen or pencil?
Scissors?
A coin?
A paper clip?
An eraser?
A spoon or fork?
A piece of wood?
This book?

Your compass can help you find iron in objects.
That's because the compass needle is really a magnet!
The needle is pulled toward anything made of iron.

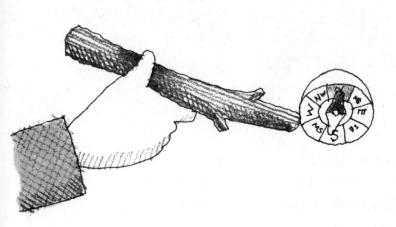

Hold the object against the compass.
Does the needle move?
If the needle stays still, the object has no iron.
Or it may be that the object has
too little iron to move the needle.
If the needle moves, the object is made of iron.

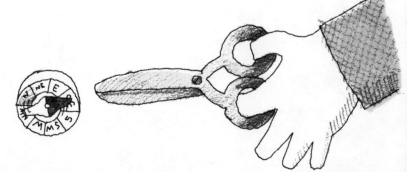

Take a short walk around the house, compass in hand.
Hold it up against different objects.
Try the stove,
- the refrigerator,
- the sink,
- the table,
- a door,
- a chair,
- the TV set,
- a bed,
and so on.
Which objects make the needle move?
They contain iron.
Which ones do not make the needle move?
They do not contain iron.

SIMPLE SCIENCE SAYS:
Solve the mystery of the compass.

The compass needle seems to move by magic.
Nothing touches it.
Yet it always points north.
Why?

The reason is that the planet Earth is a magnet.
It is one huge magnet.
Like all magnets, the earth has two poles.
One of the earth's magnetic poles is in the far north.
It is on an island in northern Canada.

The other magnetic pole is in the far south.
It is in the Indian Ocean.

You already know that your compass needle is a magnet.
And now you know that the earth is also a magnet.
Can you solve the mystery?
Can you figure out why
the compass needle always points north?

It's because the earth's north magnetic pole
acts on the compass needle.
It pulls the needle to point north.

But wait a minute.
There's something wrong!
How can the earth's *north pole* attract
the compass's *north pole?*

The basic rule of magnets says that opposite magnetic poles *attract* each other.

The north pole attracts the south pole.

The south pole attracts the north pole.

But it also says that like magnetic poles *repel,* (or push away) each other.

The north pole repels the north pole.

The south pole repels the south pole.

So why doesn't the earth's north pole *repel* the compass's north pole?

It's because the end of the compass that points north is really the south pole of the needle.

Long ago, people didn't understand magnetism.
They got mixed up.
They gave the same name
to the earth's *north* magnetic pole
and to the *north* pole of the compass.

Today many people no longer call
the point of the compass needle
the north pole.
They call it the *north-seeking* pole.
This is more accurate.
The needle *seeks* the earth's magnetic north pole.

So — that's the answer to the mystery.
What some people call the *north pole*
of the compass needle is really
the *north-seeking* (or south) pole.
It is attracted to the earth's north magnetic pole.
And that's why the compass needle always points north.

SIMPLE SCIENCE SAYS:
Make a simple compass.

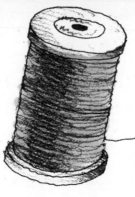

Your tiny compass is very handy.
You can put it in your pocket
and carry it around with you.

But do you know that you can also
make a compass yourself?
All you need is a bar magnet
and a length of sewing thread.

First, you have to find
the north-seeking pole of the bar magnet.
It may already be marked on your magnet.
If not, you can use your tiny compass to find
the north-seeking pole of the bar magnet.

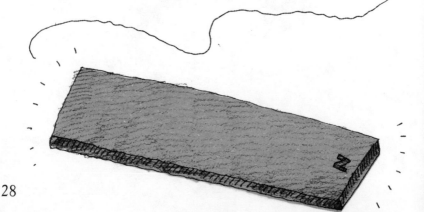

Hold one end of the bar magnet
near the red part of the needle.
Is the needle pulled toward the magnet?
Then that end of the bar magnet is the north pole.
Opposite poles attract!

Now hold the other end of the bar magnet
near the red end of the compass needle.
The needle spins around.
The red part is pushed away.
It is repelled by the magnet.
Then this end of the bar magnet
is the north-seeking (or south) pole.
Mark a dot on that end with a color marker or paint.

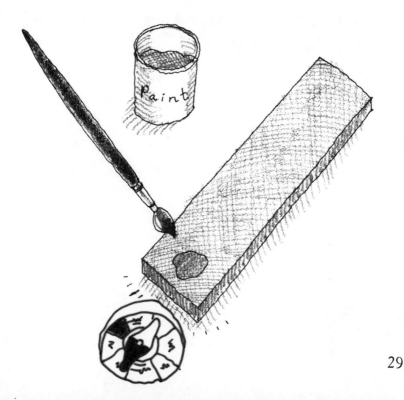

Tie one end of the thread
around the middle of the magnet.
Tie it so that the magnet is balanced.

Find a place to hang the magnet.
It should be able to swing about freely.
Keep it out of the wind, which might make it turn.

The magnet is like a compass needle.
Watch it swing back and forth.
When it stops, the north-seeking end
will be pointing north.
Compare your homemade compass
with your Simple Science compass.
Do they both point in the same direction?
What happens when you hold them next to each other?
Can you figure out why?

to the
NORTH
POLE

SIMPLE SCIENCE SAYS:
Chart the skies.

Your compass can help you find
the direction of objects in the sky.

Start with the sun.
Which direction is the sun in the morning?
Take your compass and line up north
with the point of the needle.
You'll find that the sun is
in the east.

Where is the sun in the afternoon?
The sun is in the west.
Is that what you found?

At night you can use your compass to locate the moon.
The moon rises in the east and sets in the west.
It moves across the sky just like the sun.

On a clear, dark night you can see the Big Dipper.
It is made up of seven bright stars
that form a cup and handle.
In which part of the sky did you spot it?
The Big Dipper is always to the north.
But it moves a little during the year.
In the fall and winter it is directly north
and low in the sky.
In the spring it is northeast
and high in the sky.
And in the summer it is high
and in the northwest.

SIMPLE SCIENCE SAYS:
Box the compass.

All sailors know how to "box the compass."
It means to name all the directions
of the compass from memory.

You can learn to box the compass, too.
It's easier if you make a diagram to help you.

Get a sheet of clean, unlined notebook paper.
Fold the paper in half, bottom to top.
Open it up.
Fold it in half, side to side.
Open it up.
Place it flat on a table or desk.

Use a ruler to draw lines along the folds.
The two long lines should cross
at the center of the paper.

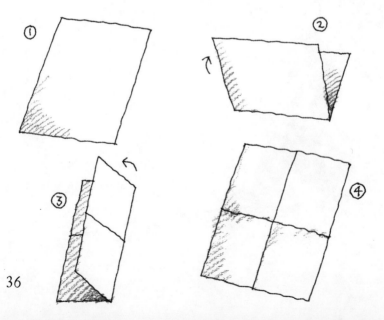

Set your compass at the point
where the lines cross.
Turn your compass so that
each cardinal point appears on a line.
Four lines should go out
from the four cardinal points.

Label the end of each line with a direction —
N for north, E for east, W for west, S for south.
Turn your paper so that N is on top.
E is then to the right.
S is on the bottom.
W is to the left.

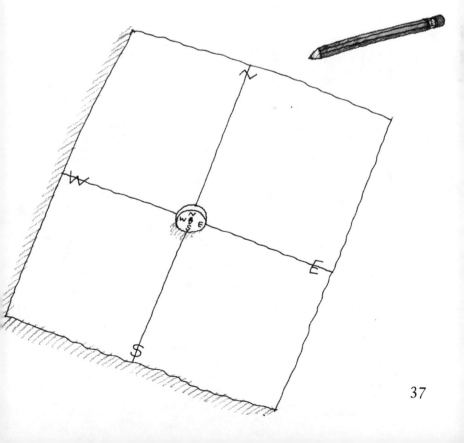

Draw the next line between south and west.
It goes from the center to the lower left-hand corner.
It points to the southwest.
Label it *SW.*

The next direction comes between west and north.
The line ends at the upper left-hand corner.
You can probably guess this direction.
Write *NW* for northwest on the line.

Now draw a line halfway between north and east.
The line goes from the center
of the paper to the upper right-hand corner.
That direction is northeast.
Mark it with the letters *NE.*

Next draw a line halfway between east and south.
This line goes from the center
to the lower right-hand corner.
Label the end of the line *SE* for southeast.

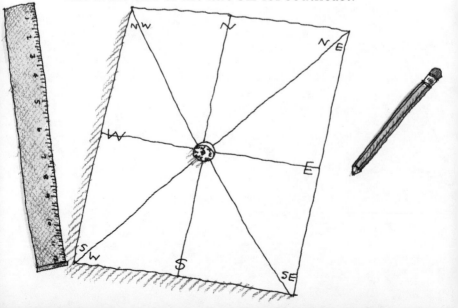

You now know the eight main points of a compass.
Can you "box the compass"
and name them all in order starting with north?
Try it.
It's easier than you think!

Learning to box the compass will —
   — help you find your way.
   — help you give other people directions.
   — help you to read maps.

N, NE, W, SW, S,

SIMPLE SCIENCE SAYS:
Map your room.

Do you know which direction your room faces?
Here's how to find out.
Stand in the room.
Hold the compass and line up north with the needle.

Is the needle pointing to a wall?
As you know, that direction is north.
That is the north wall of the room.
Write "north" on a card or piece of paper.
Attach it to the wall.

Face the north wall.
The east wall is on your right side.
The south wall is behind you.
And the west wall is to your left.
Label each wall in the room.

Suppose the needle doesn't point
straight at a wall.
It points off at an angle.
What then?
In this room, the walls are
at the intercardinal points.

Find the chart you made
when you boxed the compass.
Line the chart up with the compass.
Now you can figure out the direction of each wall.

SIMPLE SCIENCE SAYS:
Be a flight navigator.

As flight navigator it's your job
to map the route for the pilot.
Here are the stops on your cross-country flight.

Los Angeles
Las Vegas
Seattle
Denver
Kansas City
Minneapolis
Nashville
Tulsa
Dallas
Atlanta
Cleveland
New York

This map shows the cities.
Use your compass to figure out
the direction from one city to the next.

Seattle

Denver

Las Vegas

Los Angeles

Tuls

Dallas

Start at Los Angeles and follow
the order of the list on page 43.

The pilot also checks directions with ground control.
Here are the directions they gave.
Are they the same as yours?

Los Angeles — northeast to
Las Vegas — northwest to
Seattle — southeast to
Denver — east to
Kansas City — north to
Minneapolis — southeast to
Nashville — west to
Tulsa — south to
Dallas — northeast to
Atlanta — north to
Cleveland — east to
New York.

SIMPLE SCIENCE SAYS:
See the world.

Take your compass along the next time you —
— go for a long walk.
— ride in a car.
— travel on a plane or train.
— take a bike ride.
— go on a boat.

Figure out the different directions.
Notice each time you change direction.
Have the fun of knowing where you are.
Also keep from getting lost.

SIMPLE SCIENCE SAYS:
Take one compass —
and let it point the way!